DENIM FASHION PI

Create Stylish Wearables from Recycled Denim

Charles Patricia

Table of Contents

INTRODUCTION

Denim, once a symbol of durable workwear, has evolved into a versatile fabric embraced by fashion enthusiasts around the world. However, as the fast fashion industry thrives, so does the mounting waste, with denim being one of the largest contributors. To combat this environmental challenge, denim upcycling has emerged as a creative and sustainable solution. Upcycling is the process of transforming old, worn-out denim garments into new, stylish items, such as jackets, bags, and even home décor pieces. This practice not only gives new life to clothes that might otherwise end up in landfills but also encourages unique, personalized fashion. The art of denim upcycling combines innovation, craftsmanship, and environmental awareness. The appeal of denim upcycling lies in its endless possibilities. Artists and designers find inspiration in the texture, color, and wear patterns of old denim, often using distressed or frayed fabrics to create one-of-a-kind pieces. Techniques such as patchwork, embroidery, and distressing are commonly employed to add character and individuality to each item. This process allows for the customization of garments, turning something as simple as a pair of old jeans into a statement piece. The rise of denim upcycling has not only influenced the fashion world but has also sparked a larger conversation about sustainability. It encourages people to rethink their relationship with clothing and to prioritize quality over quantity. By embracing upcycled denim, consumers can contribute to reducing the demand for new materials, cutting down on waste, and minimizing the overall environmental impact of fashion. As the art of denim upcycling continues to gain momentum, it stands as a testament to the creativity and ingenuity of individuals committed to making fashion more sustainable. Through this practice, denim is no longer just a fabric but a medium for artistic expression, innovation, and environmental stewardship.

The Art of Denim Upcycling: Creativity and Sustainability

Denim, a fabric long associated with durability and timeless style, has been a staple in wardrobes around the world for decades. However, as the fashion industry has grown, so has the environmental impact of textile waste, with denim being a significant contributor. To address this issue, the art of denim upcycling has emerged as a creative, sustainable solution. This practice combines the imaginative repurposing of old denim with eco-conscious principles, offering both a new lease on life for worn-out garments and a way to reduce the carbon footprint of fashion.

What is Denim Upcycling?

Denim upcycling is the process of transforming old, used, or damaged denim garments into new, functional, and fashionable pieces. Instead of discarding worn jeans or jackets, upcycling turns these items into something unique, often blending multiple elements like fabric patchwork, embroidery, and even mixed materials. The result is a one-of-a-kind creation that carries both artistic value and a story, making it a highly personal and environmentally friendly alternative to fast fashion.

The Creative Process

The heart of denim upcycling lies in its creativity. Designers and DIY enthusiasts alike are drawn to the unique textures, colors, and wear patterns found in old denim. Each pair of jeans tells a story through its fading, tears, and creases, and upcycling allows these characteristics to be woven into new designs. Techniques like patchwork where smaller pieces of fabric are sewn together are commonly used to add visual interest and character. Embellishments such as embroidery, paint, or studs can further elevate the piece, turning a simple item into a statement of style. One of the main appeals of denim upcycling is the endless variety of creative possibilities. Whether it's crafting a new jacket from several pairs of jeans, converting an old pair of pants into a handbag, or using denim scraps for home décor

7

projects, the potential for transformation is limitless. The process fosters individuality and encourages people to think outside the box, creating something entirely new from the remnants of the old.

Sustainability in Fashion

Beyond the artistry, denim upcycling has a significant environmental benefit. The global fashion industry is one of the largest contributors to pollution, with millions of tons of textile waste ending up in landfills each year. Denim, known for its durability and heavy use of water and chemicals in production, exacerbates this issue. By upcycling, we reduce the demand for new resources, lower energy consumption, and minimize waste. The longer a garment can be used or repurposed, the less impact it has on the environment. Denim upcycling also promotes a shift in consumer habits, urging people to value sustainability over mass production. Instead of discarding old clothing in favor of the latest trends, individuals are encouraged to reimagine and rework their existing pieces. This approach not only helps to conserve resources but also encourages a deeper connection to the clothing we wear, moving away from the disposable culture that has become so prevalent.

The Future of Denim Upcycling

As sustainability continues to be a driving force in the fashion industry, denim upcycling is poised for even greater growth. The increasing demand for environmentally responsible products, coupled with a growing interest in unique, handcrafted items, makes upcycling an appealing solution for both consumers and designers. The movement is gaining momentum, from small, independent artisans to major fashion brands incorporating upcycled materials into their collections. By embracing denim upcycling, we are not just giving new life to old jeans we are redefining what it means to create and consume fashion in a way that is both creative and mindful of the planet. In a world where sustainability is more important than ever, the art of denim upcycling offers a tangible way to make a positive impact, one stitch at a time.

Why Upcycle Denim? Environmental and Personal Benefits

Denim is a beloved fabric known for its versatility and durability, but it also comes with a significant environmental cost. As the fashion industry continues to grow, so does the waste produced by discarded clothing, including denim. Upcycling denim offers a creative and sustainable solution that not only helps the environment but also provides personal benefits for those who choose to participate. Let's explore why upcycling denim is a win for both the planet and the individual.

Environmental Benefits of Upcycling Denim

Reducing Textile Waste

The fashion industry is notorious for contributing to the growing global issue of textile waste. Denim, being a sturdy and long-lasting fabric, can take years to decompose in landfills. By upcycling denim, old or damaged garments are repurposed instead of being discarded, effectively reducing the volume of waste that ends up in landfills and incinerators. This helps to minimize the environmental footprint of our clothing choices.

Conserving Natural Resources

The production of denim requires a significant amount of natural resources, such as water, energy, and cotton. For example, manufacturing one pair of jeans can use up to 2,000 gallons of water. By upcycling, the need for new resources is drastically reduced, as existing denim is reused instead of being turned into new products. This conservation of resources helps reduce the demand for raw materials, cutting down on the energy and water used in the production process.

Lowering Carbon Emissions

The environmental impact of textile production is not limited to water and energy usage carbon emissions also play a major role. Denim manufacturing, especially when it involves synthetic dyes and chemical treatments, contributes to significant greenhouse gas emissions. By upcycling denim, we can help reduce the carbon footprint associated with new garment production. Reworking existing denim eliminates the need for additional manufacturing processes, helping to curb emissions.

Promoting Circular Fashion

Upcycling is a key aspect of the circular fashion movement, which encourages the reuse and recycling of materials to create a closed-loop system in the fashion industry. This model reduces the reliance on new materials and supports the creation of sustainable, long-lasting products. By embracing upcycled denim, consumers contribute to this shift toward a more sustainable and regenerative fashion ecosystem.

Personal Benefits of Upcycling Denim

Creativity and Personal Expression: One of the most exciting aspects of upcycling denim is the opportunity to express creativity. When you upcycle old denim, you have the freedom to customize it according to your personal style. Whether it's turning a pair of jeans into a unique handbag, adding embroidery to an old jacket, or creating a completely new garment, the process allows you to showcase your individuality. Upcycled denim pieces are often one-of-a-kind, ensuring that your fashion choices stand out from mass-produced items.

Cost Savings: Upcycling can also be a cost-effective way to refresh your wardrobe. Rather than buying new denim items that can be expensive, you can breathe new life into your old jeans or jackets. With some basic sewing skills, creativity, and a few additional materials, you can transform worn-out denim into something entirely new without spending a lot of money. This approach allows you to experiment with different styles and trends without breaking the bank.

Sentimental Value and Personal Connection: Upcycling denim also provides an emotional benefit. Many people form strong attachments to their favorite jeans or denim jackets, but over time, these items may show signs of wear and tear. Upcycling allows you to retain the sentimental value of these garments while giving them a

13

new purpose. Whether it's a pair of jeans that you've worn on memorable occasions or a jacket passed down through generations, upcycling gives these items new life and makes them even more meaningful.

Encouraging Sustainable Fashion Choices: By choosing to upcycle, you become part of the larger movement toward sustainable fashion. Engaging in upcycling practices allows you to take control of your clothing consumption and make a conscious effort to reduce your environmental impact. This mindset can spill over into other aspects of life, encouraging you to adopt more sustainable habits overall, such as supporting eco-friendly brands, choosing quality over quantity, and reducing your reliance on fast fashion.

Unique and Customizable Fashion: Upcycled denim offers an opportunity for highly personalized fashion pieces. You can transform basic denim items into something entirely new, often with a level of craftsmanship and design that can't be found in store-bought garments. Whether you're adding studs, patches, embroidery, or hand-painting, the customization options are endless. This level of personalization gives you the chance to create garments that truly reflect your personality, taste, and values.

Tools and Materials for Denim Crafts

Creating denim crafts through upcycling or DIY projects can be a fun and rewarding experience. Whether you're looking to make custom clothing, accessories, or home décor items, having the right tools and materials is essential for achieving the best results. Here's a guide to some of the most useful tools and materials for denim crafts:

Essential Tools for Denim Crafts

Sewing Machine: A sewing machine is one of the most important tools for working with denim, especially if you're repurposing larger pieces like old jeans or jackets. Denim is a heavy fabric, so having a sewing machine with adjustable settings and the ability to handle thick materials will make your projects smoother and more professional.

Look for machines that offer straight and zigzag stitch options for flexibility.

Hand Sewing Needles: For smaller, detailed projects or areas where a sewing machine might be difficult to reach (like the cuffs or seams), hand sewing needles are essential. Use strong, durable needles specifically designed for heavy fabrics like denim. These needles usually have a thicker shaft and a sharp point to penetrate the fabric easily.

Denim Needles: These are specialized needles designed to handle the thickness of denim without causing damage or breaking. They have a strong shaft and a larger eye to accommodate thicker threads. Denim needles are available for both hand and machine sewing.

Fabric Scissors: A good pair of fabric scissors is a must-have for any denim craft project. These scissors are sharp enough to cut through thick denim fabric with ease. For more intricate designs, consider using smaller, precision scissors for cutting around curves or delicate details.

Rotary Cutter and Cutting Mat: If you're working on a large project that requires precise cutting, a rotary cutter can be an excellent tool. It's especially useful for cutting straight lines or making cuts on multiple layers of denim. Pair it with a cutting mat to protect your workspace and keep the blade sharp.

Pins and Fabric Clips: When working with denim, fabric pins or clips are crucial for holding pieces together before stitching. Denim is thicker and heavier than many other fabrics, so fabric clips (which don't leave holes) can be especially useful for holding bulky sections like pockets or seams.

Iron and Ironing Board: Pressing your denim before or after sewing is important to ensure clean seams and a professional finish. An iron and ironing board are essential tools for flattening hems, seams, and pockets. Be sure to use an appropriate heat setting for denim fabric to avoid damage.

Ripper (Seam Ripper): Mistakes happen, and a seam ripper will help you easily undo stitching without damaging the fabric. It's particularly helpful when making adjustments or when you need to take apart a pre-existing denim garment to upcycle it.

Embroidery Hoop: For adding decorative elements like embroidery or stitching, an embroidery hoop can hold your denim fabric taut and in place. This is especially helpful for detailed designs or patterns that require precision.

Stencil or Template: For those who want to create specific shapes or designs on denim, stencils or templates are useful tools. These can help you trace patterns, logos, or symbols onto the fabric before cutting or painting.

Materials for Denim Crafts

Old Denim Garments: The most obvious material for upcycling projects is old denim clothing, such as jeans, jackets, skirts, or shirts. Repurposing these items provides the base fabric needed to create something new and unique. Be sure to choose garments in good condition, as heavily worn denim may be too fragile for certain projects.

Denim Scraps: If you're working on smaller craft projects, denim scraps from old garments are a great material. You can cut these into shapes or strips to make patches, embellishments, or patchwork designs.

Fabric Paints and Dyes: To personalize or refresh old denim, fabric paints or dyes can be used to add color and unique designs. Fabric paint is ideal for creating artistic designs, while fabric dye is perfect for changing the overall color of a piece. Be sure to use paints and dyes that are specifically designed for use on denim and fabric.

Embroidery Floss or Thread: For embroidery or adding decorative stitching to your denim craft, embroidery floss or thick thread is essential. You can create patterns, designs, or even hand-stitched details like floral motifs or geometric shapes. For machine embroidery, use heavy-duty threads suitable for denim.

Patches and Appliqués: Patches (either iron-on or sew-on) are an easy way to add personality to denim items. You can find various pre-made patches, or create your own by cutting shapes or designs from fabric and stitching them onto the denim. Appliqué fabrics and designs can also be used to embellish denim clothing.

Rivets and Studs: Rivets and studs are perfect for adding a bit of edge to your denim projects. They're often used for reinforcing pockets or seams, but they also make excellent decorative details. Choose from a variety of finishes, including silver, gold, brass, and antique, depending on your style preference.

Denim Washers and Distress Tools: If you want to give your denim projects a distressed or vintage look, distressing tools like sandpaper, denim washers, or even a cheese grater can help you achieve the desired effect. These tools can create worn-out edges, frayed hems, and unique texture on your denim pieces.

Zippers and Buttons: Denim crafts, particularly when converting old garments into accessories or new items, often require zippers or buttons. Choose sturdy metal zippers or buttons that complement the style of your project. These can be used for adding functional elements like pockets, closures, or decorative accents.

Leather Strips or Patches: Adding leather details to denim can create a striking contrast. Leather strips or patches can be sewn onto denim for added durability or decoration. These are often used for reinforcing seams, creating labels, or adding a rustic or high-end touch to denim accessories.

Denim Fabric (New or Recycled): If you need additional denim material for your project, you can purchase denim fabric by the yard. You can choose from a variety of washes, weights, and textures to suit your specific needs. Alternatively, consider repurposing recycled denim fabric from old clothing or thrift stores.

Denim Care: How to Prepare Old Denim for Crafting

Preparing old denim for crafting is an essential step in ensuring your project turns out well. Denim, especially when repurposed from old clothing, needs to be cleaned, prepped, and sometimes altered to work effectively for crafting. Here's a guide to help you prepare old denim for your next creative project, whether it's upcycling a pair of jeans, transforming an old jacket, or repurposing denim scraps for a new creation.

1. Assess the Condition of the Denim

Before you begin any crafting project, it's important to assess the condition of the denim you're working with. Check for:

Wear and tear: Look for areas that are overly frayed, stained, or have holes. These areas might need reinforcement or creative solutions, such as patching or embroidery.

Stains: Denim can have stubborn stains, so it's essential to identify and treat them before you start crafting.

Seams and stitching: Examine the seams for any loose threads or areas that need reinforcing. Denim can fray easily, so strong stitching or additional reinforcement might be necessary for certain areas.

2. Clean the Denim

Cleaning the denim before starting your craft project is crucial, especially if it's been worn and stored for a while. Here's how to properly clean and prep it:

Wash in cold water: Denim can shrink or fade if washed in hot water, so always wash it in cold water to prevent any unexpected changes in size or color.

Use mild detergent: Denim is a durable fabric, but harsh chemicals can damage the fibers over time. Use a gentle, eco-friendly detergent to keep the fabric in good condition.

Remove stains: If there are stubborn stains, treat them before washing. For grease stains, use dish soap, and for other stains, consider a stain remover designed for fabrics. Make sure to test any cleaning products in a small, inconspicuous area before using them on the entire garment.

Air dry or tumble dry on low: Denim can become stiff if air-dried. To keep it soft, consider tumble drying on a low heat setting, or if you prefer to air dry, give it a gentle shake before hanging it.

3. Remove Zippers, Buttons, and Other Hardware

For certain projects, you may want to remove zippers, buttons, rivets, or other hardware from the denim before working with it. This can make the fabric easier to cut, sew, and reshape. Here's how:

Use pliers for rivets: If your denim piece has rivets, use pliers to remove them carefully, making sure you don't damage the fabric. You can always reuse these rivets for decorative purposes.

Detach zippers and buttons: Use a seam ripper or scissors to carefully remove zippers, buttons, and any other hardware you don't need for your project. Save these pieces for later use, as they can be incorporated into the final design or used on other upcycling projects.

4. Pre-Shrink the Denim (If Necessary)

If you're working with denim that's brand new or if you're uncertain about how much the fabric might shrink, it's a good idea to pre-shrink it before crafting. Here's how:

Wash and dry: Wash the denim on a normal cycle and dry it using your preferred method (air drying or tumble drying on low). This will allow the fabric to shrink before you start cutting and sewing.

Steam: If you're concerned about shrinkage but don't want to risk losing the fit or feel of the fabric, you can also steam the denim to help relax the fibers without causing too much shrinkage.

5. Iron or Press the Denim

Ironing or pressing denim is an important step for achieving clean, crisp seams and smooth finishes, especially if you're sewing or adding embroidery. Here's how to do it:

Set the iron to a high heat setting: Denim is a heavy fabric, so it requires a higher heat to press out wrinkles. Ensure your iron is set to the highest heat setting suitable for cotton fabrics.

Use steam for better results: Steam helps relax the fabric and makes it easier to iron. Use the steam setting on your iron or lightly spray the fabric with water before pressing.

Press carefully: Work in small sections and gently press the denim to avoid flattening out any textures you want to preserve. For seams, you can press them open to make sewing easier.

6. Cut the Denim

Once your denim is clean, dry, and pressed, you can start cutting it to suit your project. Here are a few tips for cutting denim:

Use sharp fabric scissors: Denim is thick and can dull scissors quickly, so make sure you're using a sharp pair of fabric scissors designed for cutting heavy materials.

Cut with the grain: Pay attention to the direction of the fabric grain when cutting. This helps maintain the fabric's strength and structure, particularly in areas like seams or hems.

Consider the pattern: If you're working with a specific pattern (e.g., making a new garment), make sure to follow it precisely. If you're cutting freehand, think about how the cuts will affect the finished product and the fabric's overall look.

7. Reinforce the Denim (If Necessary)

If the denim is thin or worn in certain areas, reinforcing those sections before starting your craft project can prevent future tears or issues. Here's how to do that:

Use fusible interfacing: For lightweight or worn denim, fusing an extra layer of interfacing can provide added structure and durability. Apply it to areas where the fabric may be weak or where extra support is needed (e.g., around pockets or seams).

Patch worn spots: If there are areas with holes or extensive wear, you can patch them with additional pieces of denim or other fabric. This is also a great opportunity to add creative embellishments like embroidery, appliqué, or decorative stitching.

8. Plan Your Crafting Project

Before diving into your crafting, take a moment to plan out your design. Think about how you want to transform the denim whether you're adding patches, creating a bag, making a new garment, or simply distressing the fabric. Preparing your materials and sketching out a rough idea of your project will help you stay organized and ensure that the final product is exactly what you envisioned.

Safety Tips and Crafting Best Practices for Denim Projects

Working with denim can be an enjoyable and rewarding experience, but it's essential to follow proper safety precautions and best practices to ensure both your safety and the success of your project. Whether you're using sewing machines, cutting tools, or fabric paints, following these guidelines will help you work more efficiently and safely.

Safety Tips for Denim Crafting

Use Proper Tools and Equipment

Sewing Machines: Always read the instruction manual before using a sewing machine. Ensure the needle is appropriate for denim (denim needles are designed for thick fabrics) and that the machine is properly threaded.

Sharp Tools: Tools like fabric scissors, rotary cutters, and seam rippers are sharp and can easily cause injury if not handled carefully. Always cut away from your body and fingers, and store tools safely when not in use.

Cutting Mat: When using a rotary cutter, always work on a self-healing cutting mat to prevent accidental cuts to your work surface or hands.

Wear Protective Gear

Safety Glasses: When working with tools that could throw debris, such as rotary cutters or power drills (if adding hardware like rivets), wearing safety glasses is a good idea.

Thimble: If you're hand sewing, a thimble can protect your fingers from needle pricks.

Work Gloves: For extra protection, especially when working with tough fabrics or handling hot tools like irons, wear work gloves that allow flexibility but protect your hands.

Work in a Well-Lit Area

Adequate lighting is important to avoid eye strain and ensure precision when cutting, sewing, or adding embellishments to your denim project. Ensure your workspace is well-lit to prevent mistakes and accidents.

Keep the Work Area Clean

A cluttered workspace can lead to accidents. Keep your tools, materials, and fabric organized, and regularly tidy your area to reduce the risk of tripping or losing track of important pieces. Clear away any fabric scraps, pins, or other small items from the work surface, as they can be a tripping hazard or get caught in your sewing machine.

Take Breaks

Working on denim crafts, especially if using a sewing machine or other repetitive motions, can lead to strain on your hands, wrists, and eyes. Make sure to take frequent breaks to avoid discomfort or injury.

Properly Handle and Store Materials

Fabric Paints and Dyes: Always follow the manufacturer's safety instructions for paints and dyes. Use them in a well-ventilated area and wear gloves to protect your skin.

Chemical Cleaners: If you use any fabric cleaners or stain removers, make sure they're safe for home use and that the area is ventilated. Follow the manufacturer's guidelines on usage.

Avoid Using Damaged Tools

Regularly inspect your scissors, sewing machine, rotary cutters, and any other tools for wear or damage. Using broken or dull tools can cause injuries or ruin your project.

Crafting Best Practices for Denim Projects

Pre-Wash Denim

Before starting any crafting project, always pre-wash denim to eliminate any sizing, dirt, or chemicals from manufacturing. Pre-washing also prevents any unwanted shrinking that might occur later.

Test Materials and Techniques

Before diving into your main project, test your materials (such as fabric paint, glue, or embroidery floss) on a small scrap of denim. This ensures that they adhere correctly and won't damage or stain the fabric.

Measure and Plan Carefully

Denim is a strong and durable fabric, but it's essential to plan your cuts carefully to avoid mistakes. Measure multiple times and mark your fabric with chalk or a fabric marker to guide your cuts and stitching. Always double-check your measurements before cutting.

Use a ruler or straightedge to cut straight lines, especially when working with patchwork or creating custom pieces.

Use Strong, Durable Thread

When stitching denim, use a strong, durable thread (such as polyester or cotton-wrapped polyester). Denim can be heavy and thick, so regular thread might not hold up well. Be sure to use the correct needle and thread for denim projects.

Reinforce Stress Points

Denim is a sturdy fabric, but areas that endure the most stress like pockets, hems, and seams can benefit from additional reinforcement. Use double stitching or backstitching for added strength, particularly when you're adding embellishments or alterations.

Iron and Press Seams for Clean Finish

Iron or press your denim before and after sewing to ensure clean seams and hems. This will also help ensure the fabric lies flat and has a polished look. Always check the iron's temperature settings to avoid damaging the fabric.

Creative Embellishments

Adding decorative touches such as embroidery, patches, studs, or beads can give your denim project a personalized flair. Be creative, but keep in mind that embellishments should be placed strategically so they don't interfere with the fabric's strength or comfort. If you're using fabric paint or dye, apply in light layers and allow each layer to dry completely before adding more. This will help avoid uneven finishes.

Take Care of the Finished Piece

After completing your denim craft, take steps to ensure its longevity. If it's an accessory or piece of clothing, follow the specific care instructions for washing and cleaning. For denim art or home décor, treat the fabric with fabric protector sprays to reduce stains and increase durability. Whenever possible, use scraps or leftover denim from other projects. You can repurpose smaller pieces into new items such as wallets, keychains, or decorative patches. Not only does this reduce waste, but it also adds a creative touch to your project.

Experiment and Learn

Don't be afraid to experiment with different techniques and materials. Denim crafting is a journey, and every mistake or trial offers a learning opportunity. Whether you're sewing, dyeing, or adding embellishments, exploring new ideas will keep your projects exciting and fresh.

CHAPTER ONE

GETTING STARTED WITH DENIM UPCYCLING

Denim upcycling is a fantastic way to breathe new life into old, worn-out clothing and create unique, custom pieces. Whether you're looking to make a new pair of jeans, a bag, or decorative items for your home, denim is a durable and versatile fabric that can be transformed with a little creativity and the right techniques. Here's a guide to help you get started with basic denim upcycling skills, including cutting, sewing, distressing, incorporating other materials, and essential stitches for your projects.

BASIC TECHNIQUES FOR CUTTING, SEWING, AND DISTRESSING DENIM

Cutting Denim

Sharp Scissors: Use fabric scissors or a rotary cutter to cut through denim. Denim is thick, so make sure your tools are sharp to prevent fraying and uneven edges.

Cut Along the Grain: Always cut along the grain of the fabric (in the direction the threads run). This will help the fabric maintain its strength and avoid stretching or warping.

Use a Template: If you are cutting a specific shape or pattern, use a template or a ruler for precision. For example, when making patches or smaller elements, trace your design with a fabric marker or chalk before cutting.

Pre-Wash and Dry: Before cutting, pre-wash the denim to ensure it's clean, and to prevent unwanted shrinkage once your project is completed.

Sewing Denim

Needles: Always use a denim or heavy-duty needle when sewing. These needles have a stronger shaft and sharper point, making it easier to sew through thick denim layers.

Thread: Use a durable thread, such as polyester or cotton-wrapped polyester, designed for heavy fabrics.

Denim projects need strong stitching to withstand wear and tear.

Machine vs. Hand Sewing: For large or heavy-duty projects, a sewing machine is the best choice. For more detailed work, such as hand-stitching embellishments, hand sewing is ideal. More on that below!

Distressing Denim

Sandpaper or a Grater: To achieve a distressed look, use sandpaper or a cheese grater to rub the fabric in areas where you want to create frayed edges or a worn look. Focus on areas like pockets, hems, or thighs for a natural distressed appearance.

Scissors: You can also use scissors to make small cuts and snips along seams or in areas that you want to look frayed.

Bleach or Dye: For a more dramatic distressed effect, apply bleach or fabric dye in spots to give your denim a faded, worn-in look. Be sure to wear gloves and work in a well-ventilated area when using bleach.

Using a sewing machine vs. Hand sewing for denim crafts

Sewing Machine

Pros:

Speed: A sewing machine allows you to sew large areas and multiple layers of denim quickly and efficiently.

Precision: Machines offer more precise stitches, which is especially helpful for sewing straight lines or seams that need to be strong, such as waistbands, hems, or seams.

Durability: With the right settings, sewing machines can handle multiple layers of thick denim without much difficulty.

Cons:

Setup: You need to know how to properly set up the machine, including selecting the right needle, thread, and stitch settings.

Limited Detail Work: A machine is great for large pieces, but it can be harder to control when working on detailed sections, like hand embroidery or delicate patches.

Hand Sewing

Pros:

Control: Hand sewing gives you complete control over smaller, more detailed tasks. It's perfect for adding personal touches like embroidery, decorative stitching, or patches.

Portability: No need for electricity or bulky equipment. You can easily hand-sew anywhere.

Better for Small Jobs: If you're just making minor repairs, adjustments, or embellishments, hand sewing is a great option.

Cons:

Time-Consuming: Hand sewing is slower compared to using a machine, especially for larger or heavy-duty projects.

Less Strong: Hand stitches might not hold up as well as machine stitches, especially for seams that undergo stress (e.g., crotch area of pants).

When to Use Each:

Sewing Machine: For larger, structural parts of your project like hemming, sewing seams, or creating base layers for bags, jackets, or pants.

Hand Sewing: For finishing touches like embroidery, small repairs, or adding embellishments like beads, studs, or patches.

HOW TO INCORPORATE OTHER MATERIALS (FABRIC, EMBELLISHMENTS, ETC.)

Denim upcycling is all about creativity and adding personal touches to your project. Here's how you can incorporate other materials to enhance your designs:

Adding Other Fabrics

Mixing Textures: Pair denim with other fabrics such as cotton, velvet, leather, or lace to create a unique contrast. For example, adding a velvet pocket to a pair of jeans or a cotton lining to a denim bag can add both style and function.

Patchwork: Use denim scraps or other fabric pieces to create patchwork designs. You can sew patches onto jackets, jeans, or bags to add a pop of color or texture.

Sewing Tips: When sewing denim with a lighter fabric, make sure to use the appropriate needle and stitch length. Denim is heavier, so be mindful of how it interacts with thinner fabrics.

Embellishments

Embroidery: Embroidery can be done by hand or with a machine. Floral, geometric, or custom designs can be added to pockets, cuffs, or the back of a jacket. Embroidery floss or heavy-duty thread can give your project a beautiful, textured finish.

Patches and Appliqués: Iron-on or sew-on patches are a great way to personalize your denim. Choose from pre-made designs or create your own by cutting shapes out of fabric and attaching them to the denim.

Beads, Sequins, and Studs: These embellishments can be sewn into the fabric to create a more decorative, boho, or rock-inspired look. Use a needle and thread to attach them securely in patterns or designs you like.

Leather: Adding leather elements like straps, patches, or trims can give denim a chic, rustic, or industrial feel. Leather works particularly well with denim jackets or bags.

Dyeing and Painting

Fabric Dye: Denim can be dyed in various colors to give it a fresh new look. Whether you want to darken it, make it lighter, or experiment with different hues, fabric dye works wonders.

Fabric Paint: If you want to add designs, patterns, or graphics, fabric paint is a great way to do so. Use stencils or freehand to paint unique artwork on your denim.

ESSENTIAL STITCHES FOR DENIM PROJECTS

When working with denim, it's important to use the right stitches to ensure durability and finish. Here are some essential stitches to master for denim crafting:

Straight Stitch

The basic straight stitch is the most common stitch for denim. It's used for seams and general construction. Make sure to adjust the stitch length to about 2-3 mm, as longer stitches might pull through the fabric.

Zigzag Stitch

A zigzag stitch is used to prevent raw edges from fraying. You can use this stitch on the edges of denim pieces or when attaching denim to other fabrics. It also works well for reinforcing seams.

Backstitch

The backstitch is a strong, durable stitch that can be used to reinforce seams, especially in high-stress areas like crotches or side seams. It's done by sewing backward and then forward, which creates a sturdy, locked stitch.

French Seam

This is a neat and durable way to finish seams. It encloses the raw edges of the fabric inside, preventing fraying, and gives the interior of your project a clean, professional look.

Topstitch

A topstitch is typically used on the outside of denim projects to create a decorative, strong seam. It's often done with a contrasting thread for a polished finish.

Double Stitch

For extra durability, double stitching is great for seams that take a lot of strain. You sew over the original stitching a second time to reinforce the line and ensure the fabric holds up.

CHAPTER TWO

QUICK AND EASY DENIM CRAFTS

Denim is an incredibly versatile fabric that can be upcycled into a variety of fun and functional crafts. Whether you have old jeans, jackets, or fabric scraps, you can create stylish and sustainable items for yourself, your home, or as gifts. Here are some quick and easy denim craft ideas to get you started.

1. Denim Patches: Repairing and Personalizing Clothing

Denim patches are a fantastic way to repair worn or torn clothing while adding a personalized touch. You can use denim to cover up holes, add decorative elements, or give old garments a new life.

How to Make and Use Denim Patches:

Cut the Patch: Cut a piece of denim that's slightly larger than the hole or tear. You can use an old pair of jeans or leftover fabric scraps.

Prepare the Area: If you're using a patch for a hole, trim the frayed edges around the tear. For a neat look, fold the edges under before attaching the patch.

Attach the Patch: You can either hand sew or use a sewing machine to stitch the patch in place. Use a simple straight stitch or zigzag stitch for reinforcement. If you want a quicker fix, iron-on patches are also a great option.

Add Embellishments: For a personalized touch, you can add embroidery, beads, or fabric paint to the patch to make it truly unique.

This method works for jeans, jackets, bags, and even shoes, making it a versatile solution for upcycling.

2. Denim Coasters: A Simple Craft for Home Décor

Denim coasters are easy to make and add a rustic, chic touch to your home décor. They are practical, stylish, and can be personalized to match your space.

How to Make Denim Coasters:

Cut the Denim: Cut circles or squares from old denim jeans or scraps. A good size for coasters is around 4-5 inches in diameter.

Reinforce the Fabric: Denim can fray, so you might want to reinforce the edges by folding them under and stitching around the perimeter, or using a zigzag stitch to prevent fraying.

Optional: Add extra layers of fabric to the back for a thicker, more absorbent coaster. Felt or cork fabric works well for this.

Embellish: You can leave the coasters plain or add embroidery, fabric paint, or decorative stitching for a unique design.

These coasters make a great addition to any coffee table and are a perfect way to repurpose old denim.

3. DIY Denim Bracelets and Accessories

Denim isn't just for clothing it's also great for creating accessories like bracelets, belts, and headbands. Denim bracelets are especially easy to make, and you can customize them with your own style.

How to Make Denim Bracelets:

Cut Strips: Cut denim strips from old jeans. The strips should be about 1-2 inches wide, depending on how thick you want the bracelet.

Braiding or Twisting: You can either braid three strips together or twist two strips to create texture. Secure the ends with fabric glue or sew them to ensure they stay in place.

Add Embellishments: Add beads, charms, or buttons to the denim strips for a decorative touch. You can also stitch on patches or use fabric paint for a unique design.

Closure: Add a button or snap to close the bracelet or tie it off with a knot. These denim bracelets can be worn alone or layered with other accessories for a boho-chic look.

4. Upcycled Denim Keychains and Bag Charms

Repurposing denim into keychains or bag charms is a fun and easy craft that requires minimal materials. These items make excellent gifts or personal accessories and can be customized with different shapes and embellishments.

How to Make Denim Keychains or Bag Charms:

Cut Shapes: Cut out fun shapes or rectangles from denim scraps hearts, stars, circles, or any design you prefer.

Reinforce: If you want your keychain or bag charm to be sturdy, reinforce the denim by doubling it up or attaching a felt backing.

Add a Key Ring or Clip: Sew or glue a key ring or a lobster clasp onto the top of your denim shape to turn it into a keychain or bag charm.

Decorate: Use embroidery, buttons, fabric paint, or small charms to embellish your design. For added flair, add a tassel or beads. These little denim creations are not only functional but also stylish, adding a personalized touch to your keys, bags, or backpacks.

5. Denim Headbands and Hair Accessories

Denim headbands and hair accessories are a trendy and eco-friendly way to update your wardrobe. They're easy to make, customizable, and perfect for both casual and dressy occasions.

How to Make Denim Headbands:

Cut the Denim: Cut a long strip of denim that's about 2-3 inches wide and long enough to fit around your head (usually 16-18 inches).

Create the Band: Fold the edges of the denim strip over to create a smooth, finished edge. Sew along the sides or use fabric glue to secure the edges.

Add Elastic: To make the headband stretchy, sew a small piece of elastic at the ends of the denim strip. This will help the headband stay in place and adjust to fit your head.

Embellish: Add a bow, flowers, or beads to the center of the headband to make it more decorative. You can also embroider or paint on the denim to add personal flair. These denim headbands are a stylish accessory for any outfit and are perfect for both casual wear and special occasions.

CHAPTE THREE

DENIM FASHION PROJECTS

Denim is a versatile fabric that can be transformed into a variety of stylish and unique fashion items. Whether you're looking to update your wardrobe, try a new DIY project, or give new life to old denim, there are countless ways to repurpose jeans, jackets, and other denim pieces. Here are some creative denim fashion projects that are both fun to make and wear.

1. Turning Old Jeans into Stylish Skirts and Dresses

Repurposing old jeans into skirts or dresses is a fantastic way to create new wardrobe staples from fabric you already have. Whether you're aiming for a casual look or something more dressy, denim skirts and dresses can be easily customized to your style.

How to Make a Denim Skirt:

Cut the Jeans: Start by cutting the legs off your jeans to the desired length for your skirt. You can either make a mini, midi, or full-length skirt depending on your preference.

Shape the Skirt: If you want a more tailored fit, you can take in the sides of the jeans to give them a more flattering shape. If you prefer a looser fit, you can leave the sides as they are.

Create a Skirt Shape: Sew the inner thigh area shut, and then add a waistband using the top of the jeans or fabric from another pair of denim. You can also add a zipper or button closure at the back.

Distressing (Optional): For a more distressed look, use sandpaper, a cheese grater, or scissors to create frayed edges or worn patches on the skirt.

How to Make a Denim Dress:

Repurpose the Jeans and Jacket: Use an old pair of jeans for the bottom part of the dress and a denim jacket or shirt for the top. Simply sew the top and bottom pieces together, adjusting the fit as needed.

Add a Waistband: If you'd like a more fitted look, you can add a denim belt or sew the dress tighter at the waist. Add buttons or a zipper to the back for closure. These denim skirts and dresses are not only fashionable but also give new life to items you might have otherwise discarded.

2. DIY Denim Jackets: Customizing and Embellishing

A classic denim jacket is a wardrobe essential, but a DIY customized version allows you to add a personal touch and make it truly one-of-a-kind. Whether you're adding embellishments, patches, or a new fit, denim jackets are an easy and fun project.

How to Customize a Denim Jacket:

Add Patches: Iron-on or sew on patches of your choice floral, band logos, animal prints, or even custom designs. Patches can be placed on the back, sleeves, or front for a personalized look.

Paint and Embroidery: Use fabric paint to create designs, or try your hand at embroidery for a delicate touch. Whether it's flowers, geometric patterns, or text, embroidery adds texture and color to your jacket.

Distress the Fabric: If you want a vintage or worn look, lightly distress the fabric by using sandpaper or a cheese grater. Focus on areas like the collar, cuffs, and seams.

Add Studs or Rhinestones: Add a bit of edge to your denim jacket with metal studs, rhinestones, or spikes. Attach them to the shoulders, cuffs, or back for a bold, rock-inspired look.

Change the Fit: If your denim jacket is oversized or too small, you can take it in to create a more fitted look, or add extra fabric to make it more relaxed or longer.

3. Recycled Denim Shorts: A Summer Staple

Denim shorts are a must-have in the summer, and turning an old pair of jeans into stylish shorts is an easy project that takes only a few steps. Whether you want a trendy, frayed pair or a clean, tailored look, denim shorts are a great way to recycle old jeans.

How to Make Denim Shorts:

Cut the Jeans: Start by cutting your jeans to the desired length for shorts. You can make them long, mid-thigh, or super short based on your preference.

Distress the Edges: If you like a frayed look, use scissors or a cheese grater to distress the edges of the shorts. For a clean finish, fold the edges under and sew them to create a hem.

Add Embellishments: For a fun twist, you can add fabric paint, embroidery, or studs to personalize your denim shorts. You could also replace the buttons or add lace trim to give them a fresh look. These recycled denim shorts are perfect for hot weather and can be styled in various ways, from casual to boho-chic.

4. Upcycled Denim Bags: Totes, Purses, and Backpacks

Old denim can be repurposed into trendy, durable bags. Whether you're making a simple tote, a stylish purse, or a functional backpack, denim is the perfect fabric for crafting bags that are both eco-friendly and fashionable.

How to Make a Denim Tote Bag:

Cut Denim Panels: Use the legs of old jeans to create the panels for your tote bag. You'll need two pieces for the front and back, as well as a bottom piece.

Sew the Pieces Together: Sew the front and back panels together, then sew the bottom piece onto the sides to create the bag shape. Add handles made from denim strips, fabric, or leather.

Decorate: Add embellishments like embroidery, fabric paint, or patches to give your tote bag a unique look. You can also use contrasting fabric for the lining and inner pockets.

How to Make a Denim Purse or Backpack:

Purse: Use a denim jacket or a pair of jeans as the main body of the purse. Add a zipper closure, interior pockets, and a strap made from denim or fabric.

Backpack: For a denim backpack, you can use the legs of jeans for the body and create straps from the waistband or other denim scraps. Add zippers or buttons to secure the bag and make it functional. Upcycled denim bags are not only fashionable but also sturdy and practical for everyday use.

5. Denim Shoes and Sandals: Upcycling Footwear

Transform old denim into unique, custom footwear. Whether you want to make sandals, sneakers, or denim slip-ons, denim can be used to create comfortable and stylish shoes that are perfect for summer.

How to Make Denim Shoes or Sandals:

Denim Sandals: Upcycle an old pair of flip-flops by covering the straps with denim. You can either glue or sew denim pieces to the straps for a fresh look. Add embellishments like beads, sequins, or studs to make your sandals stand out.

Denim Slip-ons: If you have an old pair of slip-on shoes or sneakers, you can cover them with denim fabric to give them a new look. Cut and glue denim to the sides of the shoes, then use fabric paint or embroidery for decoration.

Customize Existing Shoes: Use denim to create decorative elements for existing shoes, like patching up worn spots, adding a denim bow, or attaching a denim flower to the front. Denim shoes are an excellent way to showcase your creativity and add a personalized touch to your footwear collection.

CHAPTER FOUR

HOME DÉCOR PROJECTS WITH DENIM

Denim is a durable and versatile fabric that doesn't just belong in your wardrobe. It can also be repurposed into stylish and functional home décor items that add a cozy, rustic, or modern touch to your space. By using old jeans, jackets, or fabric scraps, you can create one-of-a-kind pieces that are both sustainable and chic. Here are some creative home décor projects that make use of denim:

1. Denim Pillows: Creating Cozy Throw Pillows

Denim throw pillows are a great way to add texture and style to your living room, bedroom, or any space in need of some cozy accents. Denim's sturdiness makes it perfect for pillows that will stand up to everyday use while adding a touch of rustic charm.

How to Make Denim Pillows:

Cut the Fabric: Start by cutting denim into two squares or rectangles of equal size. You can use old jeans, denim jackets, or fabric scraps. The size will depend on your desired pillow dimensions, but typically 16-18 inches is a good size.

Sew the Pillow Together: Place the two denim pieces together with the right sides facing inward. Sew around the edges, leaving one side open for inserting the pillow form or stuffing.

Insert the Filling: Turn the pillow case right side out, then insert a pillow form or fill it with stuffing. Sew the opening closed using a hand stitch or a machine.

Add Embellishments: For a unique look, you can add details like embroidery, patches, or fabric paint. You can also combine different denim shades to create a patchwork effect. These denim pillows will add a rustic, cozy vibe to your couch or bed while providing comfort and style.

2. Denim Throw Blankets and Quilts

Denim throw blankets or quilts are a great way to use up old denim and create a cozy, functional piece for your home. Whether you're looking for something warm to drape over your sofa or a stylish bedspread, denim quilts provide both comfort and durability.

How to Make a Denim Throw Blanket or Quilt:

Cut the Denim: Start by cutting denim into squares, rectangles, or strips. You can mix different washes of denim or use denim from different items to create an interesting, varied design.

Arrange the Pieces: Lay out the denim pieces on the floor or a large table in your desired pattern. You can go for a patchwork design, stripes, or a more modern geometric layout.

Sew the Pieces Together: Using a sewing machine, stitch the denim pieces together, row by row. Once all the rows are completed, sew them together to create the full blanket.

Add a Backing: For a soft and cozy backing, choose a fabric like flannel or cotton. Sew it to the quilted denim, leaving a small border to show off the denim edges.

Finish the Edges: Use a zigzag stitch or a bias tape to finish the edges of the quilt for a clean and durable finish. This upcycled denim quilt or throw blanket is perfect for adding warmth and texture to your living space or bedroom.

3. Upcycled Denim Curtains and Window Treatments

Denim curtains can add a rustic, industrial, or casual vibe to your windows. Denim's thickness also provides some privacy and light-blocking properties, making it a great option for window treatments.

How to Make Denim Curtains:

Measure Your Windows: First, measure the length and width of your windows to determine how much denim fabric you'll need. You may want to use old jeans or larger denim garments to make the most of the fabric.

Cut the Denim: Cut the denim pieces to the size needed for your window. You can mix and match different washes of denim to create a unique design.

Create the Hem: Fold the edges of the denim to create a clean hem, and then sew it down. If you want to avoid hemming, you can leave the edges raw for a more rugged look.

Add Curtain Rod Pockets or Loops: To hang the curtains, sew a pocket at the top of the fabric to slide a curtain rod through, or add fabric loops for a more decorative touch.

Personalize with Patches or Embellishments: To make your denim curtains more unique, add fabric patches, embroidery, or even denim appliqués for extra texture and interest. These upcycled denim curtains are not only functional but will also add a cool, casual style to any room.

4. Denim Wall Hangings and Art: Framing Denim for Display

Denim isn't just for furniture or textiles it's also an excellent material for creating wall art. Whether framed as a single statement piece or used in a patchwork design, denim wall hangings are an easy way to add character to any room.

How to Make Denim Wall Art:

Frame Denim Pieces: Start by cutting denim into interesting shapes or patterns, such as squares, rectangles, or circles. You can use old jeans, jackets, or even patches for this project.

Create a Patchwork Design: Arrange the denim pieces on a canvas or board to form a patchwork design. Use fabric glue to secure the pieces, or sew them in place if you want a more textured look.

Add Embellishments: For extra interest, you can add embroidery, fabric paint, or decorative stitching to the denim. Try adding quotes, images, or simple patterns for a modern touch.

Frame and Display: Once your denim art is finished, frame it in a simple wooden frame or create a hanging system to display it on the wall. These denim wall hangings provide a unique, creative way to showcase your upcycled denim while adding personality to your home décor.

5. Denim Rugs: Weaving and Braiding for Unique Flooring

Denim is a durable fabric that can also be used to create beautiful, textured rugs. Whether you're braiding, weaving, or stitching, denim rugs are a great way to repurpose fabric scraps while adding a functional and stylish element to your flooring.

How to Make a Denim Rug:

Cut the Denim: Cut your denim into strips. You can use old jeans, jackets, or other denim fabric. The size of the strips will depend on the type of rug you want to create (wider strips for a chunky rug, narrower strips for a more detailed design).

Braiding or Weaving: To create a simple braided rug, braid three strips of denim together and sew the braids into a spiral or oval shape. For a woven rug, you can use a basic weaving technique, creating a grid pattern with the denim strips.

Sew the Pieces Together: Once you've created enough braided or woven sections, sew them together using a strong, durable thread. You can stitch them into a circle, rectangle, or another shape that suits your space.

Add a Backing: For added durability and comfort, add a non-slip backing to your denim rug. You can use fabric glue or sew a piece of felt, canvas, or rubber backing to the underside of the rug.

These denim rugs add warmth, texture, and a unique design element to any room, from the living room to the entryway.

CHAPTER FIVE

ECO-FRIENDLY AND SUSTAINABLE DENIM PROJECTS

Denim is not only a fashionable fabric but also a sustainable one when repurposed creatively. By upcycling old denim into functional, eco-friendly items, you can reduce waste while contributing to a greener planet. Whether you're making reusable shopping bags, planters, or stylish home accessories, denim offers countless possibilities for eco-conscious crafting. Here are some sustainable denim projects to try:

1. Denim Shopping Bags and Reusable Totes

With the increasing need for eco-friendly shopping alternatives, denim makes an excellent material for crafting durable, reusable shopping bags and totes. By repurposing old jeans or denim jackets, you can create functional, stylish bags that reduce plastic waste.

How to Make a Denim Tote Bag:

Prepare the Denim: Start by cutting out pieces from old jeans, jackets, or denim scraps. You'll need two large pieces for the front and back of the tote and additional fabric for the handles.

Sew the Bag: Place the front and back pieces together with the right sides facing inward and sew along the sides and bottom. Turn the bag right side out.

Make the Handles: Cut two long strips of denim for the handles. Attach them securely to the top edges of the tote bag.

Add Personal Touches: You can embellish your bag with embroidery, fabric paint, or even denim patches for a more customized look. These denim tote bags are not only functional for grocery shopping or carrying books but also a sustainable alternative to single-use plastic bags.

2. Denim Planters: Creating Stylish Plant Holders

Old denim can be transformed into unique planters that not only showcase your creativity but also contribute to reducing fabric waste. Denim planters add a rustic or industrial feel to your home décor while helping your plants thrive.

How to Make Denim Planters:

Cut the Denim: Use old jeans or denim fabric to cut out pieces large enough to wrap around a small plant pot. You can use one piece for the base or multiple strips for a patchwork design.

Create a Pot Cover: Wrap the denim around your plant pot, leaving enough extra fabric to tuck in at the top. Use a hot glue gun, fabric glue, or a simple stitch to secure the fabric.

Add Personalization: For extra flair, you can add embellishments like lace trim, fabric paint, or embroidery to give your denim planter a unique look. You can also line the inside with plastic to protect the denim from moisture. Denim planters are an ideal way to upcycle your old clothing and create one-of-a-kind containers for your plants.

3. Upcycled Denim for Gift Wraps and Packaging

Denim can be repurposed to create sustainable and stylish gift wraps that are both practical and eco-friendly. By using old denim to wrap gifts, you eliminate the need for disposable wrapping paper while adding a personal touch to your presents.

How to Make Denim Gift Wraps:

Cut the Denim: Use old denim clothing or scraps and cut them into squares large enough to wrap around your gift.

Wrap the Gift: Place your gift in the center of the fabric and fold the edges around it. You can tie the package with denim strips, fabric ribbons, or jute twine to keep it secure.

Personalize the Wrap: Add fabric patches, embroidery, or paint to make the denim gift wrap even more special. You can also create a fabric tag using denim and write a personal message. This project not only saves money on gift wrap but also helps you reduce your environmental footprint.

4. Denim Storage Bins and Organizers

Repurposing denim into storage bins and organizers is a practical way to give old fabric a new life while reducing clutter in your home. These denim bins are both sturdy and stylish, making them a great choice for organizing toys, books, or office supplies.

How to Make Denim Storage Bins:

Cut the Denim: Start by cutting your denim into panels that can be sewn together to form a box shape. You can use the legs of old jeans or a denim jacket.

Sew the Panels: Sew the sides and bottom of the panels together to create a box-like structure. To add structure and durability, you can use an old cardboard box as a base or insert a piece of fabric stiffener.

Create Handles: Add handles by cutting strips of denim and sewing them onto the sides of the bin.

Customize: For added organization, consider adding internal dividers made of denim or another fabric. These upcycled denim bins help keep your home organized while reducing the need for plastic containers.

5. Denim Coasters, Mats, and Trivets for Eco-conscious Homes

Denim is a durable fabric that can be upcycled into useful home accessories like coasters, mats, and trivets. These practical items can protect your surfaces while offering a sustainable, eco-friendly alternative to disposable options.

How to Make Denim Coasters and Mats:

Cut Denim Strips: Start by cutting denim into strips or squares for your coasters or mats. The number of strips or squares will depend on how large you want your final product to be.

Weave or Sew Together: For coasters, you can weave the denim strips together in a basket-weave pattern, or simply sew the squares together for a patchwork effect. For mats and trivets, you can sew the denim pieces in a spiral or grid pattern.

Add Layers for Durability: To make your coasters and mats more durable, sew several layers of denim together. This provides extra padding and ensures they can withstand heat.

Personalize: Add embellishments like embroidery, fabric paint, or patches for extra flair. These denim coasters and trivets are not only eco-friendly but will add a rustic, homemade charm to your kitchen or dining area.

CHAPTER SIX

CREATIVE DENIM CRAFTING TECHNIQUES

Denim is a versatile fabric that allows for endless creativity. Whether you're looking to add color, texture, or personal flair, there are many techniques you can use to elevate your denim projects. By experimenting with dyeing, embroidery, distressing, and more, you can turn your old denim pieces into unique, custom creations. Here are some creative denim crafting techniques to try:

1. Dyeing and Painting Denim for Custom Colors and Designs

Dyeing and painting denim is an easy and fun way to give your fabric a completely new look. Whether you want to achieve a solid color, create an ombré effect, or add intricate designs, these techniques will allow you to personalize your denim projects.

Dyeing Denim:

Choose the Right Dye: You can use fabric dye, which is available in various colors, or natural dyes made from plants, fruits, and vegetables for a more eco-friendly approach.

Prepare the Denim: Wash the denim to remove any dirt or oils, and then prepare the dye according to the instructions. Submerge your denim in the dye bath, and let it soak until you achieve your desired shade. For a more even color, make sure to stir the fabric regularly.

Rinse and Dry: After dyeing, rinse the denim in cold water to remove excess dye and set the color. Hang the denim to dry, or dry it in the dryer for a softer feel.

Painting Denim:

Fabric Paint: Use fabric paint to create custom designs on your denim. You can use a paintbrush or a fabric marker to draw patterns, phrases, or even freehand artwork.

Stencils: For more precise designs, use stencils or masking tape to create geometric shapes or floral patterns on your denim.

Heat Set the Paint: Once your design is complete, heat set the paint using an iron to ensure it doesn't wash out. This technique is perfect for creating custom-colored denim items or for adding a personalized touch to any project, such as jackets, jeans, bags, or accessories.

2. Adding Embroidery, Beading, and Appliqué to Denim

Embellishing denim with embroidery, beading, and appliqué allows you to add texture, dimension, and personal style to your creations. These techniques are great for enhancing denim jackets, jeans, bags, or even home décor items like pillows.

Embroidery:

Simple Stitches: Start with basic embroidery stitches like running stitch, backstitch, or satin stitch to create floral designs, patterns, or personalized monograms.

Intricate Designs: For more detailed designs, you can use techniques like French knots, chain stitches, or even cross-stitch to create eye-catching motifs.

Use Thread and Needle: Choose embroidery floss or heavy-duty threads that contrast with the denim for a striking effect. If you want a subtle look, use colors that complement the denim.

Beading:

Adding Beads: Beads can be sewn onto your denim project to create unique accents. Sew them along seams, around pockets, or in patterns like flowers or abstract designs.

Embellishment Areas: Popular areas to add beads include the collar of a jacket, the cuff of pants, or as decorative elements on bags and accessories.

Appliqué:

Fabric Appliqué: Cut out shapes from different fabrics, and sew them onto the denim to create layered designs. This is perfect for adding floral patterns, animals, or custom logos to your projects.

Iron-on Appliqué: For a faster method, use iron-on appliqué to add shapes, symbols, or patches to your denim without sewing. These techniques will elevate your denim creations and allow you to incorporate unique designs and textures.

3. Denim Shredding and Distressing Techniques for a Vintage Look

Distressing and shredding denim is a popular technique for giving fabric a worn, vintage appearance. Whether you're looking to add subtle fraying or create bold tears and holes, these methods will give your denim a more personalized and rugged aesthetic.

Shredding and Fraying:

Fray the Edges: Use a seam ripper or sandpaper to gently fray the edges of your denim, such as the hem of jeans, the cuffs of sleeves, or the waistband of a jacket.

Distressed Pockets: For a more distressed look, use scissors or a rotary cutter to make small slits and then pull out threads with a tweezer, leaving frayed edges.

Sandpaper: Rub sandpaper on specific areas of your denim, such as knees, thighs, or around seams, to create a worn-in, faded effect. This method works well for both a subtle look and more aggressive distressing.

Creating Holes:

Strategic Rips: Use a pair of fabric scissors or a craft knife to cut slits in areas where you want holes. Then, use a pair of tweezers to pull out threads to create an authentic distressed look.

Use a Razor Blade: For a more authentic worn look, run a razor blade over the surface of the denim in places like the knees or thighs to create small, shredded areas.

Wash and Dry: After distressing, wash your denim item to soften the fabric and allow the distressing to become more pronounced. These distressing techniques help create that perfect "vintage" look, whether you're working on jeans, jackets, or skirts.

4. Creating Patches and Embellishments from Denim Scraps

If you have leftover denim scraps, you can easily turn them into custom patches and embellishments that can be added to other denim items or used for new crafting projects. This method is both eco-friendly and cost-effective.

How to Make Denim Patches:

Cut Denim Scraps: Cut out different shapes or sizes from your denim scraps, such as hearts, stars, circles, or more intricate designs.

Add Details: Use embroidery, fabric paint, or beads to decorate the patches. This will give them more personality and help them stand out when applied to your projects.

Attach the Patches: You can sew the patches onto your denim item using a simple straight stitch, or you can iron them on if they have adhesive backing.

Layer and Layer Again: Combine multiple denim patches for a fun, layered look. This method is great for customizing jackets, backpacks, or jeans. Creating your own denim patches allows you to use up scraps while adding a unique touch to your clothing or accessories.

5. Using Denim for Mixed Media Art Projects

Denim's rugged texture and versatility make it an excellent material for mixed media art projects. You can combine denim with other materials such as fabric, paper, wood, and even metal to create unique art pieces.

How to Incorporate Denim into Mixed Media:

Collage Art: Cut denim into different shapes and use it as part of a larger collage. Layer the denim pieces over paper, cardboard, or canvas to create texture and depth.

Sculpture: For more dimensional art, you can stitch denim into 3D shapes or use it as part of a larger sculpture. Denim can be used to create everything from wall hangings to small tabletop sculptures.

Paint and Stitch: Combine fabric paint and stitching on a canvas, adding denim to create textured backgrounds or as part of the design.

Denim and Wood: Incorporating denim into wood-based projects, such as picture frames, shelves, or jewelry boxes, can give the piece a rustic and industrial look. Mixed media art projects allow for limitless creativity, and denim adds a unique, tactile element to your artwork.

CHAPTER SEVEN

ADVANCED DENIM UPCYCLING PROJECTS

Denim is a durable, versatile fabric that can be creatively repurposed into high-impact, functional, and artistic projects. If you've mastered basic denim upcycling and are looking to challenge yourself with more advanced techniques, there are a variety of ways to incorporate denim into furniture, home décor, and large-scale art installations. These projects can turn everyday items into statement pieces, showcasing your creativity and commitment to sustainability. Here are some advanced denim upcycling ideas to inspire your next craft venture:

1. Making Denim Furniture Covers and Slipcovers

Repurposing denim to create furniture covers or slipcovers is a great way to upcycle old jeans or jackets into functional and stylish home décor. Denim's durability makes it a perfect material for protecting your furniture while giving it a unique, custom look.

How to Make a Denim Furniture Cover:

Choose Your Denim: Use old jeans, jackets, or denim fabric for your project. For larger pieces like sofas or chairs, you may need multiple pairs of jeans or several yards of denim fabric.

Measure and Cut: Measure the dimensions of your furniture, then cut your denim pieces accordingly. Be sure to add extra fabric for seams and hems.

Sew the Pieces Together: Use a sewing machine or hand-sew the denim pieces together to create a fitted slipcover. Depending on the piece, you may need to make separate sections for the back, sides, and cushions.

Add Details: For a more personalized touch, add decorative elements like topstitching, pockets, or even custom patches from other fabric scraps.

Finish the Edges: To ensure the cover fits snugly, finish the edges with a fabric hem or use a hidden stitch to avoid fraying. Denim slipcovers can completely transform old, worn-out furniture and offer a stylish and eco-friendly alternative to purchasing new covers.

2. Upcycling Denim into Larger Art Installations

Denim can be used to create large-scale art installations that make a bold statement in any space. Whether you're working with a gallery, a community space, or your home, denim provides a unique texture and color for contemporary, mixed-media artworks.

How to Create a Denim Art Installation:

Prepare the Denim: Collect a variety of denim pieces in different shades of blue, or dye them to achieve the desired effect. Consider using different textures, such as distressed denim or smooth, untouched fabric.

Cut and Shape: Cut the denim into various shapes, such as squares, strips, or even abstract forms. You can create large-scale collages by stitching or gluing the pieces together on a canvas, wood panel, or large fabric surface.

Layer and Arrange: Arrange the denim pieces into patterns or scenes that reflect your artistic vision. Layer different pieces to create depth or use a gradient technique to give the installation an ombré effect.

Add Other Materials: For a mixed-media effect, combine denim with other materials like paper, metal, or wood. You can even incorporate lighting or 3D elements to make the piece interactive.

Install the Artwork: Hang the installation on a wall, suspend it from the ceiling, or display it as a freestanding piece in a gallery or your home. Creating large denim art installations is an excellent way to showcase your artistic vision while highlighting the sustainability of upcycled materials.

3. Denim Upholstery: Turning Old Jeans into Furniture Upholstery

If you're looking for an advanced project that transforms your furniture in a major way, consider reupholstering chairs, ottomans, or sofas with denim. This project requires more skill and patience but results in a beautifully unique piece of furniture that combines the durability of denim with the comfort of soft upholstery.

How to Reupholster with Denim:

Choose a Piece of Furniture: Select a piece of furniture that needs a makeover, such as a chair, couch, or footstool. Make sure the fabric is worn or outdated to justify the upcycle.

Remove Old Upholstery: Carefully remove the old fabric and padding from the furniture, being mindful of how it is constructed. Save the old fabric as a pattern if needed.

Measure and Cut Denim: Measure the sections you'll need to cover, adding extra fabric for seams and tacking. Cut denim fabric accordingly, making sure you have enough to wrap around the frame and cushion areas.

Upholster the Furniture: Use a staple gun to attach the denim fabric to the furniture frame. Start at the corners and work your way around, ensuring the fabric is stretched taut and even.

Reattach Cushions: For pieces with cushions, cut and sew denim covers for each cushion. Use a strong fabric or foam to ensure the cushions are comfortable and well-padded. Denim upholstery creates a bold, stylish statement while extending the life of your furniture, making it a highly rewarding and sustainable project.

4. Creating Denim Lampshades and Lighting Fixtures

Upcycling denim into lampshades and lighting fixtures is a unique way to incorporate this fabric into your home décor. Denim's sturdy structure provides a great base for creating innovative, custom light fixtures that can be used to enhance any room.

How to Make a Denim Lampshade:

Create a Frame: Start by constructing a simple wire or plastic frame for your lampshade. You can use an existing lampshade as a template, or make your own from scratch.

Cut Denim: Cut strips or panels of denim to fit the frame. Make sure the pieces are large enough to cover the entire surface of the lampshade.

Attach Denim to the Frame: Attach the denim pieces to the frame using a hot glue gun, fabric glue, or by sewing them into place. For a more layered look, you can sew two or more strips of denim together to create a textured effect.

Add Embellishments: Customize the lampshade by adding fabric patches, embroidery, or beading for a personal touch. You can also paint the denim with fabric paint for a pop of color. This project allows you to turn a functional object into an art piece while adding a cozy, rustic ambiance to your home.

5. Customizing Denim with Leather, Lace, and Other Textiles

Combining denim with other textiles such as leather, lace, silk, or cotton can elevate your upcycled denim projects and give them a unique, high-fashion look. By blending materials, you can create truly custom and one-of-a-kind pieces that express your personal style.

How to Combine Denim with Other Fabrics:

Leather: Denim and leather make a stylish, tough combination. You can add leather accents to a denim jacket, such as a leather collar, sleeve cuffs, or patches. For a bag or purse, use denim as the main fabric and leather for the straps, bottom, or details.

Lace: Lace adds a delicate contrast to the rugged nature of denim. Consider adding lace trim to denim skirts, jackets, or bags. You can also use lace in combination with denim for decorative overlays on pillows or wall hangings.

Silk or Cotton: Use softer fabrics like silk or cotton to complement denim in projects like custom quilts, throw pillows, or clothing items. Mixing these fabrics can create a balance of textures that's both sophisticated and eco-friendly.

Sewing Techniques: Combine the fabrics using different sewing techniques such as topstitching, patchwork, or appliqué to ensure a secure and durable finish. Use a sewing machine with the appropriate needle for heavy fabrics like denim and leather. This project is great for those who enjoy experimenting with mixed textures and creating fashion-forward, customized items.

CHAPTER EIGHT

UPCYCLING DENIM FOR KIDS AND BABIES

Upcycling denim for kids and babies offers a creative and sustainable way to repurpose old denim while making adorable, functional items for little ones. Denim is a durable and versatile fabric, making it ideal for creating baby clothes, kids' accessories, and home décor that can withstand the wear and tear of everyday life. Below are some great upcycling ideas for transforming old denim into fun, unique items for children:

1. Denim Baby Clothes: Upcycled Rompers and Pants

Upcycling denim into baby clothes is a great way to create sturdy, fashionable garments for your little one. Denim rompers, pants, and dresses are perfect for babies because of denim's durability and ability to withstand the messes and rough play that come with early childhood.

How to Make Denim Baby Clothes:

Rompers: Start by selecting a pair of old jeans or denim jackets. Cut the denim to size for the baby, using a pattern or measurements that fit their age group. You can add snaps or buttons for easy dressing and undressing.

Baby Pants: Turn old jeans into baby pants by cutting them into smaller sizes. Add an elastic waistband for comfort, and trim the legs to the right length. For extra style, use contrasting fabric for the inner waistband or pocket trim.

Denim Dresses: For baby girls, old denim shirts or pants can be reworked into cute dresses. Cut the fabric into a skirt shape, and add straps made from the remaining fabric. You can embellish the dress with pockets or fabric flowers for a personalized touch. These projects are not only fun but also practical for dressing babies in something unique and eco-friendly.

2. Kids' Denim Art Projects: Pouches, Wallets, and Pencil Cases

Turning denim into creative accessories is an excellent way to encourage kids to engage in DIY crafting while also teaching them the value of upcycling. Pouches, wallets, and pencil cases made from denim can be both functional and stylish.

How to Make Denim Pouches, Wallets, and Pencil Cases:

Pouches: Cut denim into small rectangles and sew them into pouches. You can add a zipper or fabric flap for closure. Personalize with patches, buttons, or embroidery.

Wallets: For older kids, transform denim into a simple wallet by cutting pieces for the front and back. Sew them together, leaving space for a foldable section. Add compartments for coins, cards, or ID tags.

Pencil Cases: Denim is a great fabric for making durable pencil cases. You can repurpose denim scraps to sew small pencil holders or even make a pencil roll-up by stitching small denim pockets in a line. These simple projects teach kids basic sewing skills while giving them a tangible product they can use daily.

3. Denim Quilts and Blankets for Children

Denim quilts and blankets are perfect for kids, offering comfort, warmth, and a personal touch. By using old denim jeans, jackets, and shirts, you can create a cozy and stylish quilt that your child will love for years to come.

How to Make a Denim Quilt:

Collect Denim Pieces: Gather old denim in varying shades of blue. You can use entire pieces of denim or cut them into squares, rectangles, or strips.

Sew the Pieces Together: Arrange the denim pieces in a pattern of your choice. You can create a checkerboard design, a patchwork style, or any custom layout you prefer. Sew the pieces together using a strong, durable stitch.

Add a Lining: For extra softness, add a flannel or cotton backing to the quilt. This will make it cozy for napping and sleeping.

Quilt the Layers: Once the pieces are sewn together, you can quilt the layers by hand or machine to keep the fabric in place and add texture. This is a larger, more advanced upcycling project that results in a beautiful and functional keepsake for your child.

4. DIY Denim Stuffed Animals and Toys

Upcycled denim can be used to create adorable, soft toys for kids, such as stuffed animals or dolls. These toys make thoughtful, handmade gifts and are a sustainable alternative to mass-produced toys.

How to Make Denim Stuffed Animals or Toys:

Choose Your Toy Pattern: Start with a simple stuffed animal pattern, such as a bear, bunny, or elephant. You can find patterns online or create your own.

Cut the Denim Pieces: Use old denim to cut out the shapes needed for the stuffed toy. Denim can be a bit stiffer than other fabrics, so consider adding a soft lining, such as cotton or flannel, to make the toy cuddlier.

Sew the Pieces: Sew the denim pieces together, leaving space for stuffing. Add buttons or fabric for the eyes and nose, and stuff the toy with soft filling material.

Embellish: Customize your stuffed toy with additional embellishments, such as denim patches, embroidered patterns, or fabric accents. These denim toys not only make great playtime companions but also encourage children to appreciate the value of handmade, upcycled items.

5. Upcycled Denim Kids' Backpacks and School Gear

Backpacks and school gear are essentials for children, and upcycling denim into these items makes for both functional and eco-friendly solutions. By using denim's durability and unique style, you can create one-of-a-kind backpacks, lunch bags, or even pencil holders.

How to Make a Denim Backpack:

Select a Denim Base: You can use an old pair of jeans or a denim jacket as the base fabric for the backpack. Cut and sew the denim to form the body of the backpack, making sure to add enough fabric to create straps and pockets.

Add Pockets: Repurpose the pockets from jeans to create external or internal compartments for added functionality.

Create Adjustable Straps: Cut strips of denim to create adjustable straps. You can also repurpose a belt or old fabric from other clothes for the straps.

Embellish and Personalize: Add custom patches, embroidery, or even fabric paint to make the backpack uniquely yours. You can also sew on a patch with the child's name for a personalized touch.This project is a great way to create a personalized school bag that is sturdy enough for everyday use.

CHAPTER NINE

GIFT IDEAS: UPCYCLED DENIM FOR SPECIAL OCCASIONS

Upcycling denim is a wonderful way to create thoughtful, sustainable, and personalized gifts for friends, family, and loved ones. Whether you're celebrating a birthday, holiday, or wedding, denim offers endless possibilities for crafting unique presents and decorations. By turning old denim into something new and meaningful, you can give gifts that are not only eco-friendly but also full of creativity and love. Here are some fantastic upcycled denim gift ideas for various occasions:

1. DIY Denim Gifts for Friends and Family

Upcycled denim makes for fun and meaningful gifts for birthdays, holidays, or just to show appreciation to your loved ones. Whether it's a cozy home décor item, a handy accessory, or a stylish piece of clothing, denim can be transformed into something special.

Gift Ideas:

107

Denim Pillows: Sew old denim into cozy throw pillows. You can personalize them with fabric paint, embroidery, or even patchwork.

Denim Tote Bags: A simple yet practical gift, denim tote bags are perfect for carrying groceries, books, or even as a beach bag. You can add personalized touches like custom embroidery or fabric patches.

Denim Coasters: Cut denim into small squares and stitch them into coasters. Add a decorative touch by embroidering a fun design or monogram.

Denim Wallets: Create durable and unique wallets by cutting and sewing denim into functional designs. Customize with colorful fabric or contrasting leather. These denim gifts are practical, stylish, and meaningful ways to repurpose old denim into something useful and personal.

2. Creating Denim Holiday Decorations and Ornaments

Upcycled denim can make delightful holiday decorations and ornaments, giving your seasonal décor a unique and sustainable touch. Denim's durability and timeless style make it perfect for holiday crafts that will last for years to come.

Gift Ideas:

Denim Christmas Ornaments: Cut denim into festive shapes like stars, hearts, or snowflakes. Sew them together, stuff with cotton, and hang them on your tree with a ribbon. For added flair, add buttons, beads, or lace.

Denim Stockings: Create a stylish and eco-friendly Christmas stocking by sewing denim into a simple pattern. Decorate the stockings with embroidery, sequins, or denim patches.

Denim Garland: Cut denim into small flags or triangles, then string them together to make a festive garland. Hang it across your mantelpiece or along a wall for a rustic touch during the holidays. These denim decorations can brighten up your holiday season while offering a personal, handmade feel.

3. Upcycled Denim Jewelry for Unique Gift Ideas

Denim jewelry is a creative way to repurpose fabric scraps into wearable pieces of art. Denim can be transformed into stylish necklaces, bracelets, earrings, and even rings that make perfect gifts for friends or family.

Gift Ideas:

Denim Bracelets: Cut denim into strips and braid them together to form stylish bracelets. Add charms, beads, or buttons for a personalized touch.

Denim Earrings: Cut small pieces of denim into circles, squares, or other shapes, then attach them to earring hooks. You can embellish the denim with embroidery, fabric paint, or rhinestones for added flair.

Denim Necklaces: Use denim strips or fabric beads to create trendy necklaces. Layer different shades of denim for a boho-chic look, or add leather accents for a more polished design. Denim jewelry is a unique, sustainable gift that reflects your thoughtfulness and creativity.

4. Personalized Denim Gifts: Monograms and Custom Designs

Personalizing denim gifts by adding monograms, names, or custom designs gives them an extra special touch. Whether it's for a birthday, anniversary, or just to show someone you care, personalized denim gifts are meaningful and memorable.

Gift Ideas:

Monogrammed Denim Pouches: Sew small denim pouches and embroider the recipient's initials on them. These pouches are perfect for storing makeup, jewelry, or small essentials.

Custom Denim Jackets: Take an old denim jacket and personalize it with the recipient's name, favorite design, or patches. You can embroider their initials or favorite quote on the back for a unique, customized look.

Denim Bags with Custom Patches: Create a custom denim tote or crossbody bag, then personalize it with fabric patches, iron-on designs, or custom embroidery. This is a great gift for someone who loves one-of-a-kind accessories. Personalizing denim items makes them even more special and unique, ensuring the gift feels personal and thoughtful.

5. Denim Wedding Crafts: Eco-friendly Ideas for Brides and Grooms

Denim can play a significant role in wedding décor and gifts, offering a rustic, eco-friendly, and stylish alternative to traditional wedding materials. From bridesmaids' accessories to decorations, denim can add a unique touch to a couple's special day.

Gift and Craft Ideas:

Denim Wedding Favors: Create small denim pouches or bags to hold wedding favors like chocolates or small keepsakes. Add personalized tags or embroidery to each pouch to make it extra special.

Denim Bridal Accessories: For the bride or bridesmaids, you can make custom denim accessories like hairbands, sashes, or even garters. Add lace, beads, or embroidery for a sophisticated touch.

Denim Wedding Guest Book: Create a guest book with a denim cover. Embellish it with embroidered initials, wedding date, or other meaningful details. You can even add fabric scraps from the wedding dresses or accessories to make it more personal.

Denim Bouquet Wrap: Instead of traditional ribbons, wrap the wedding bouquet stems in denim fabric.

Embellish with lace, pearls, or buttons to add a personal touch.

Denim "Something Blue": Use denim as part of the "something blue" tradition by incorporating it into the bride's dress, shoes, or accessories. A small denim patch sewn into the dress or hidden in the bouquet can serve as a meaningful and sustainable option. Upcycled denim crafts make the wedding day more personal and environmentally friendly while offering guests a creative and meaningful experience.

CHAPTER TEN

MAINTAINING YOUR DENIM CREATIONS

Upcycled denim items are a sustainable and creative way to give new life to old fabric, but like all crafted items, they require proper care to ensure their longevity and maintain their beauty. Whether you're working with denim clothing, home décor, or accessories, taking steps to care for your denim creations will help them last for years to come. Here are essential tips for maintaining, repairing, and storing your upcycled denim projects.

1. How to Care for Denim Upcycled Items

Caring for your upcycled denim items is crucial to keeping them looking great and lasting a long time. Denim is a durable fabric, but it still requires some attention to maintain its strength and appearance, especially when it's been upcycled and used in different ways.

General Care Tips:

Washing Denim: Always check the care instructions on your denim creation before washing. In general, denim items should be washed in cold water to prevent fading and shrinkage. If your project includes embellishments (like embroidery or beads), hand-washing or placing the item in a delicate laundry bag is recommended.

Avoid Excessive Washing: Denim doesn't need to be washed after every use. Over-washing can wear out the fabric faster. Spot clean when possible and only wash denim when it's truly dirty.

Drying: Air-drying is the best way to dry denim items. Lay them flat or hang them to avoid shrinking, especially if your upcycled piece is a garment like jeans or a jacket. If you must use a dryer, do so on a low heat setting to preserve the fabric's integrity.

Ironing: Denim can wrinkle, so ironing may be necessary for items like bags, jackets, or home décor. Set the iron to a medium heat setting, and use a pressing cloth to avoid direct contact between the iron and delicate parts like embellishments or painted designs. By taking proper care, your upcycled denim items can stay functional and fashionable for a long time.

2. Repairing and Revamping Older Denim Crafts

As with any crafted item, upcycled denim creations may show signs of wear over time. The good news is that repairing and revamping older denim crafts is usually easy, thanks to the versatility of denim and the many ways you can update it.

Repair Tips:

Patchwork: If your denim item has a tear or hole, consider adding a decorative patch. Use contrasting fabrics, embroidery, or even another piece of denim to cover the damaged area. This will not only fix the issue but also add a stylish, personalized touch.

Sewing Loose Stitches: Denim items, particularly those that have been upcycled into bags or clothing, may have loose stitches over time. Regularly check for any loose threads and use a sewing machine or needle and thread to reinforce seams.

Re-dyeing: If your denim creation has faded, consider re-dyeing it. Denim can be dyed back to a deep blue or other colors using fabric dye. This works especially well for larger items like jackets, quilts, or home décor. Be sure to follow dyeing instructions carefully to avoid uneven coloring.

Adding New Embellishments: To revamp your denim item, add new decorative elements like fabric patches, lace, beads, or embroidery. This can breathe new life into older pieces and make them feel fresh again. Revamping older denim crafts is not only practical but can be a fun opportunity to give your creations a personal upgrade.

3. Storing Denim Craft Projects for Longevity

Proper storage of your upcycled denim items will help maintain their shape, color, and overall condition. Whether your items are home décor, accessories, or clothing, good storage habits are key to ensuring they last for many years.

Storage Tips:

Keep Denim in a Cool, Dry Place: Store your denim items in a cool, dry environment to avoid exposure to excessive moisture, which can lead to mildew or fabric deterioration. Avoid storing denim in direct sunlight, as this can cause fading over time.

Use Garment Bags for Clothing: If you're storing upcycled denim clothing, such as jackets, skirts, or pants, consider hanging them in garment bags. This will protect them from dust, dirt, and potential damage. For delicate items, using padded hangers will help maintain their shape.

Fold Denim Accessories Carefully: For accessories like upcycled denim bags, wallets, or pillows, fold them carefully and store them in boxes or drawers. Avoid overstuffing to preserve their shape. You can also use cotton bags to protect these items from dust.

Store Denim Quilts and Home Décor: Denim quilts or larger home décor pieces should be folded neatly and stored in a breathable fabric storage bag or container. Make sure the items are clean and dry before storing to prevent odors or stains from setting in. By following proper storage practices, your denim creations will stay in excellent condition and be ready to use when you need them.

4. Preventing Wear and Tear in Upcycled Denim

To ensure your upcycled denim projects stand the test of time, prevention is key. While denim is a sturdy fabric, upcycled items can experience wear and tear faster than brand-new denim if not properly cared for.

Preventive Measures:

Reinforce High-Stress Areas: Denim is durable, but areas that experience frequent friction (like seams, corners, or straps on bags) can start to wear out quicker. Reinforce these areas by sewing extra stitches or adding a layer of fabric for added strength.

Avoid Overloading: If you've upcycled denim into bags, backpacks, or purses, avoid overloading them with heavy items. Excess weight can strain the fabric and seams, causing them to wear out prematurely.

Protect from Sharp Objects: Sharp objects like keys, pens, or jewelry can scratch or puncture denim, so be mindful of what you store in your upcycled denim creations. Use liners inside bags or storage pockets to reduce friction and protect the fabric.

Regular Maintenance: Inspect your upcycled denim items regularly for signs of wear. Address small repairs early to prevent them from turning into larger issues. Taking time to fix loose stitches or minor tears will extend the life of your creations. By being proactive, you can reduce wear and tear and ensure that your upcycled denim items last for many years to come.

CONCLUSION

EMBRACING THE ART OF DENIM UPCYCLING

As we move further into an era of sustainability, upcycling denim has become more than just a trend—it's a creative and eco-conscious way to breathe new life into old fabric, reducing waste while adding personal flair to everyday items. From clothing and accessories to home décor, the possibilities for upcycling denim are endless. Embracing this art form not only nurtures our creativity but also encourages mindful consumption and thoughtful craftsmanship.

Final Thoughts on Embracing Sustainable Crafting

Sustainable crafting, especially through denim upcycling, allows us to take a step toward reducing the environmental impact of our consumption habits. By giving old jeans, jackets, and other denim items a second life, we're not only preventing waste from entering landfills but also making a positive impact on the planet. Upcycled denim crafts are a wonderful way to engage in slow fashion and sustainable home décor while showcasing personal style and creativity. Embracing sustainable crafting offers a chance to move away from mass production and disposable culture, embracing the idea that items crafted with care and thought are often far more meaningful. The process of transforming denim into something new is both an art and a statement—one that aligns creativity with environmental responsibility.

Finding Your Own Denim Upcycling Style

One of the best things about denim upcycling is that it offers limitless opportunities for personalization and self-expression. Whether you prefer bold, colorful embellishments or subtle, rustic designs, there's no wrong way to upcycle denim. Start by exploring simple techniques like adding patches or embroidery, and as your skills grow, experiment with more advanced projects like denim furniture or custom fashion pieces.

Finding your unique denim upcycling style is a journey. You may be drawn to creating cozy home décor pieces, crafting stylish accessories, or even revamping entire wardrobes. The key is to have fun with the process, explore different ideas, and let your creativity lead the way. As you experiment and discover what excites you, your personal touch will become evident in every denim creation you craft.

Inspiring a New Wave of Eco-Conscious Creativity

Denim upcycling represents a movement that goes beyond just crafting it's about inspiring a culture of eco-conscious creativity. By sharing our upcycled denim projects, ideas, and techniques, we encourage others to explore sustainable practices and challenge the throwaway mentality. The more we embrace upcycling, the more we can inspire others to think about how they too can turn waste into something beautiful, functional, and meaningful. As we continue to cultivate creativity with recycled materials, we foster a community that values sustainability and craftsmanship. Whether it's teaching others, sharing your creations online, or simply showing the world how great upcycled denim can be, each small effort contributes to a larger movement of conscious creativity. By embracing denim upcycling, we can help shape a future where sustainability is at the heart of fashion, home décor, and DIY culture. In the end, upcycling denim is more than just a craft it's a powerful way to express creativity, reduce environmental impact, and inspire others to think differently about the materials they use. With endless possibilities, the art of denim upcycling offers a chance to make a difference, one stitch at a time.

Printed in Dunstable, United Kingdom

70867679R00071